This Book

Belongs to:

____

- -

____

Aa

is for

Airplane

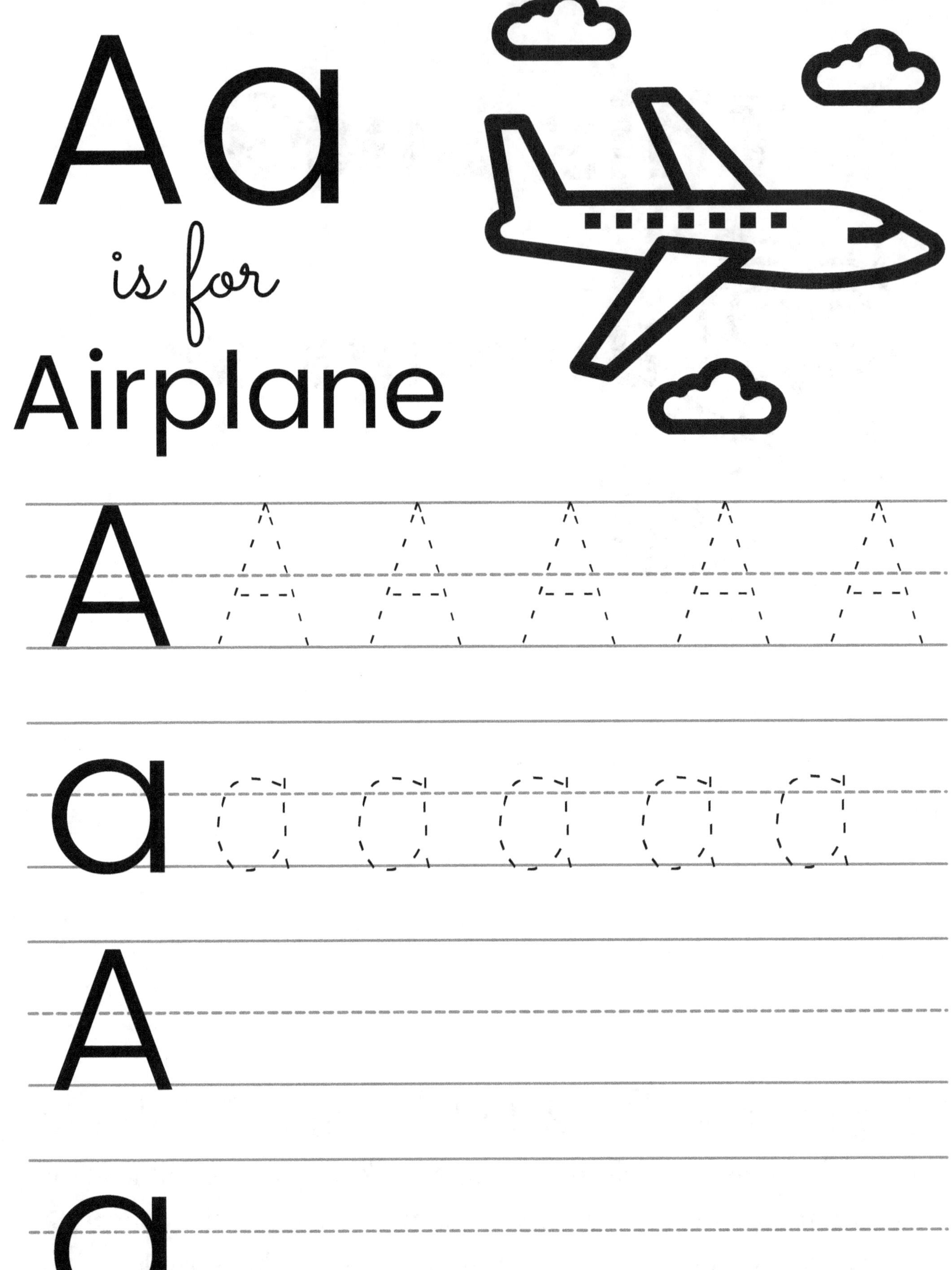

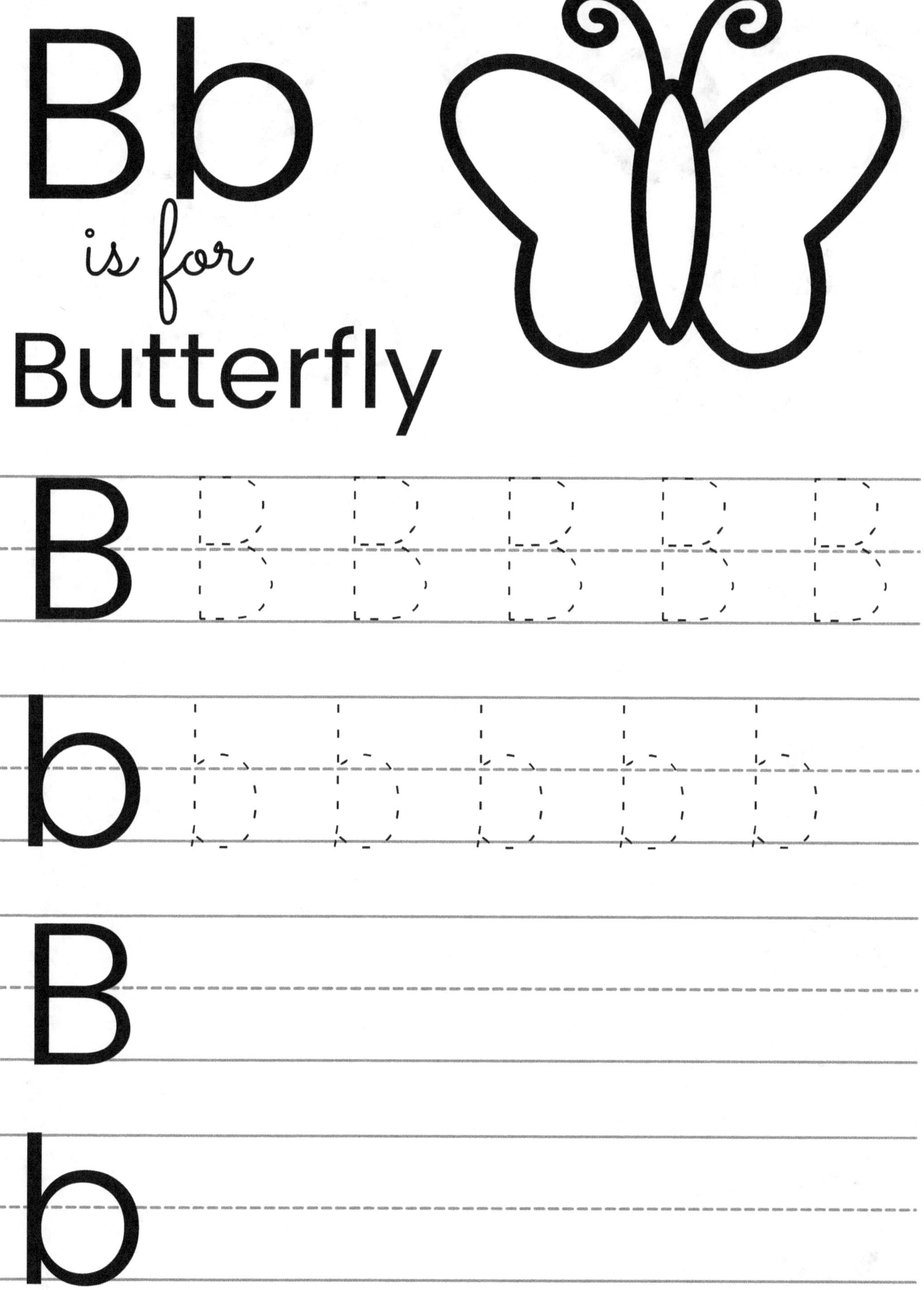

C c
is for
COW
C c c c c c c c c c
C c c c c c c c c
C
C

Dd

Dinosaur

D
d
D
d

Ee
is for
Elephant

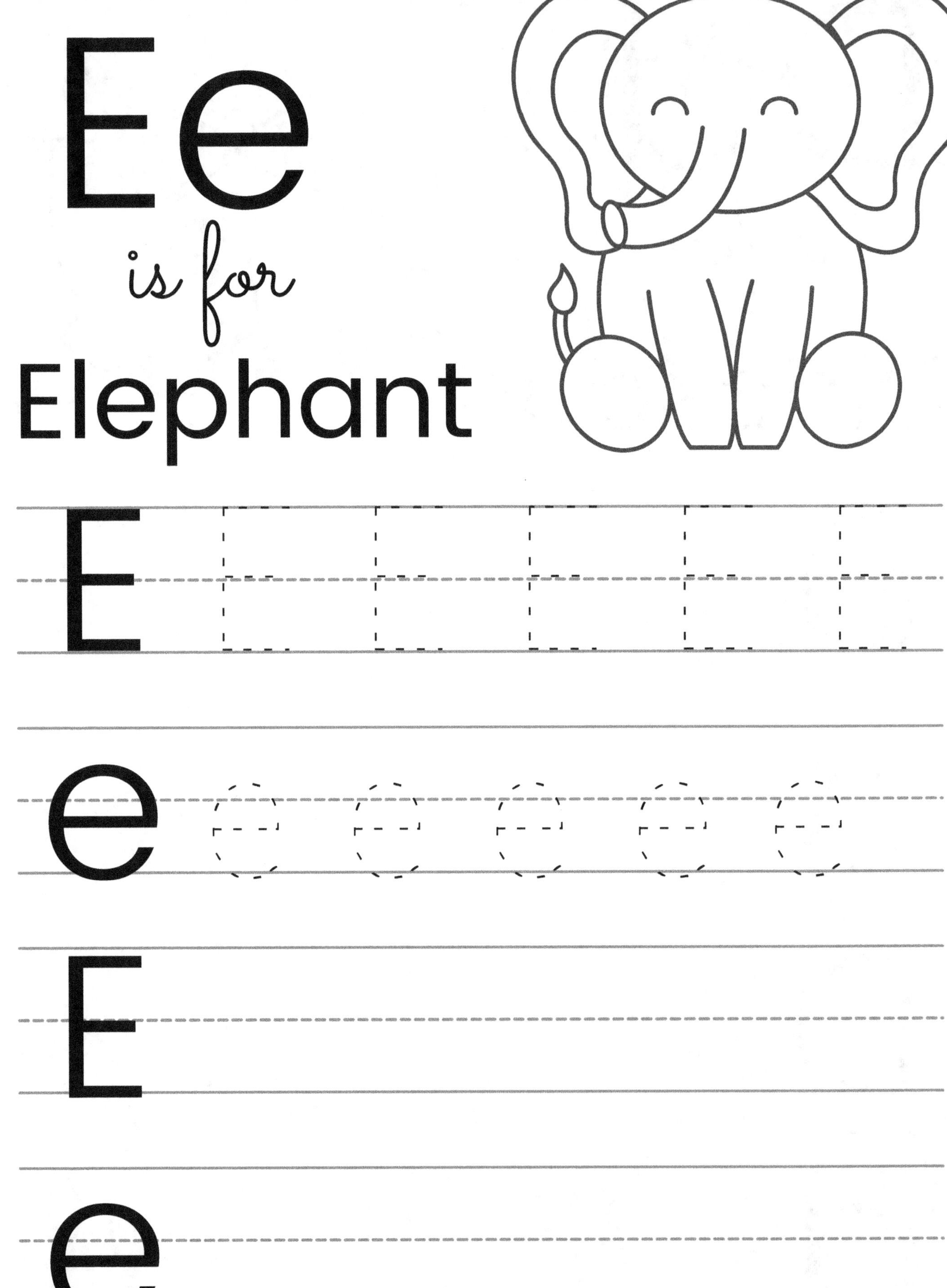

F f

is for

Flower

F

f

F

f

Gg

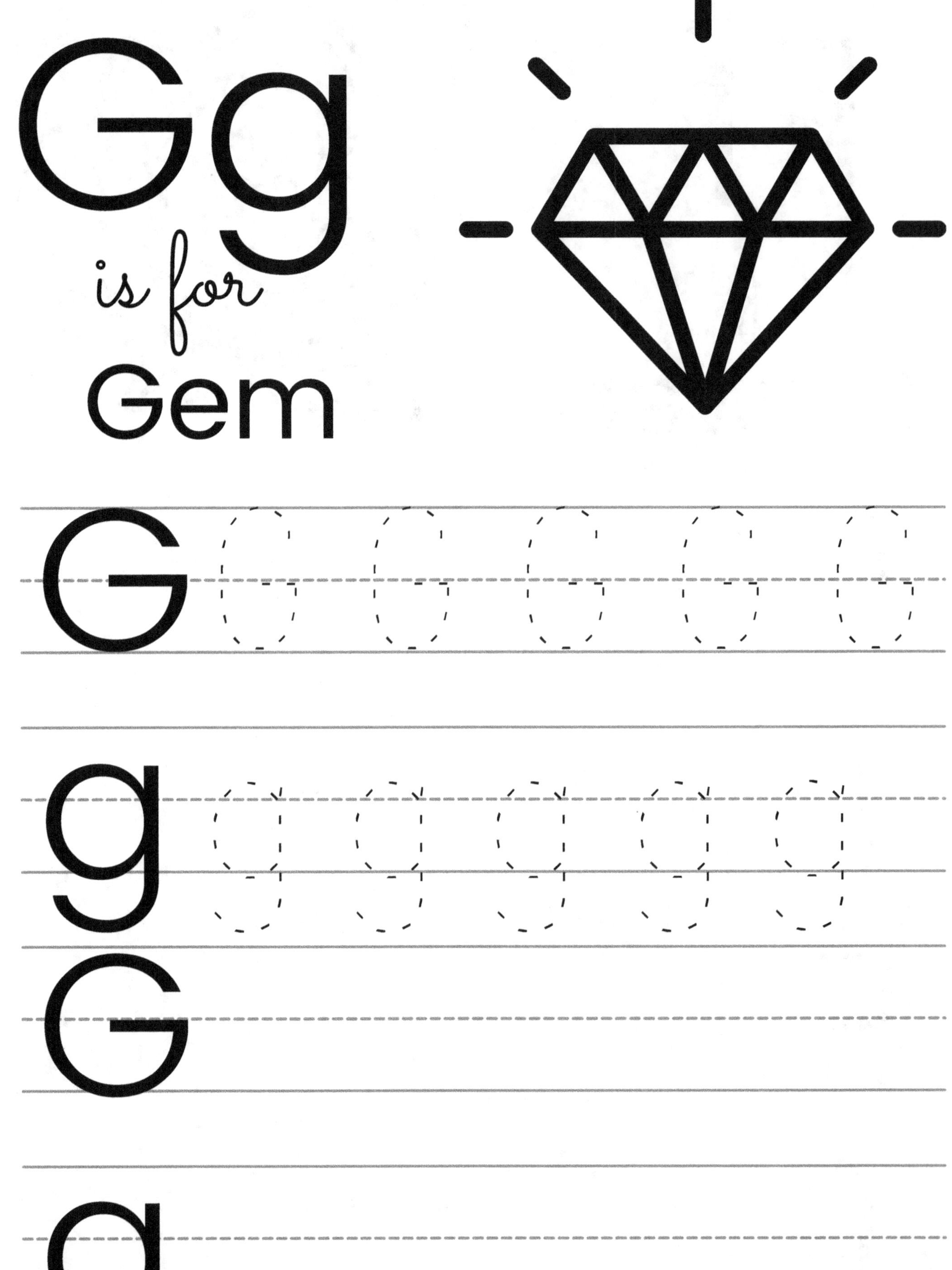

Hh

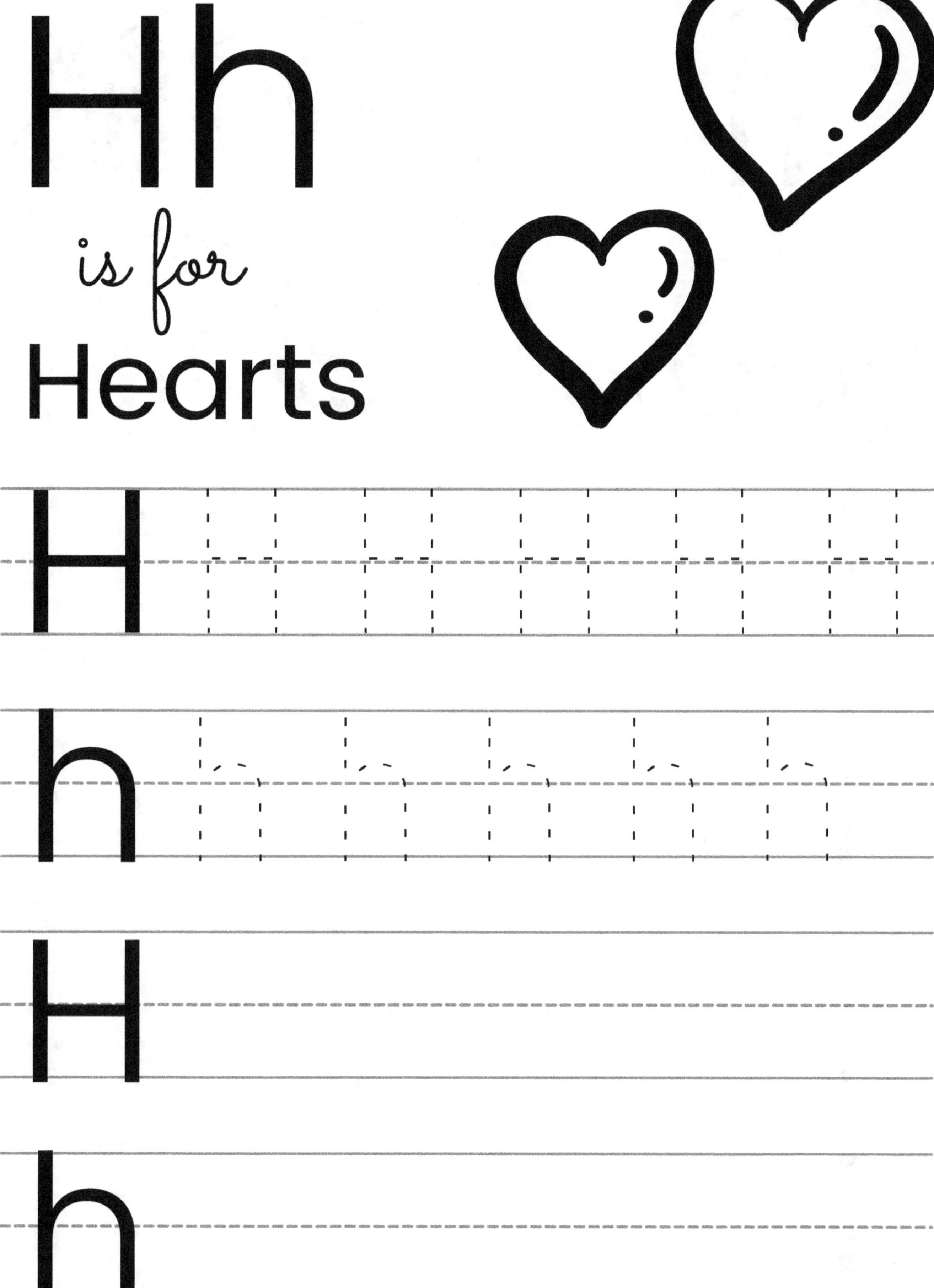

Ii

is for

Iguana

Jj
is for
Jaguar

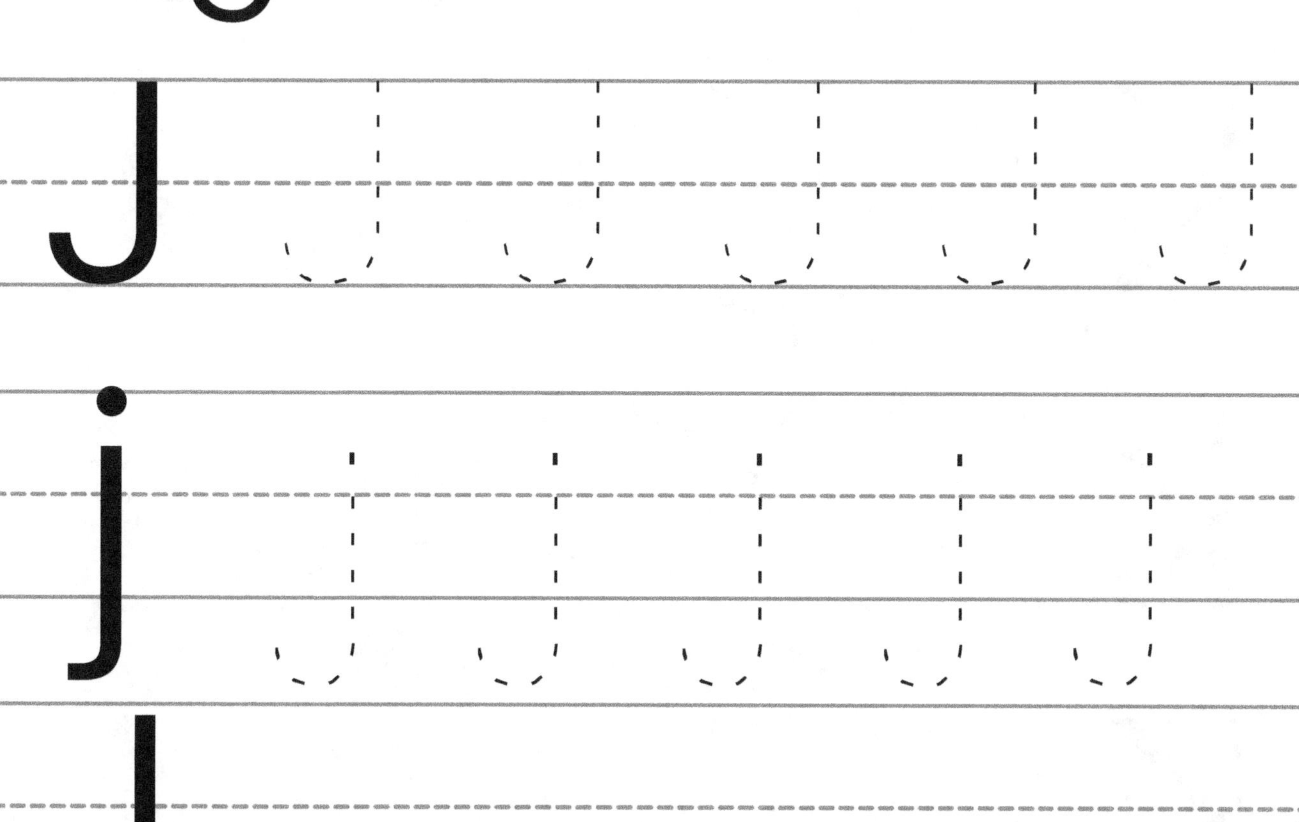

Kk

is for

Koala

K

k

K

k

L l
is for
Leaf

Mm

Monster Truck

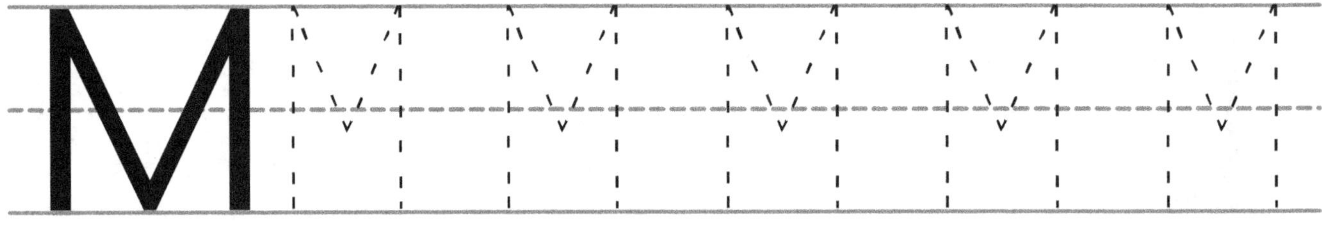

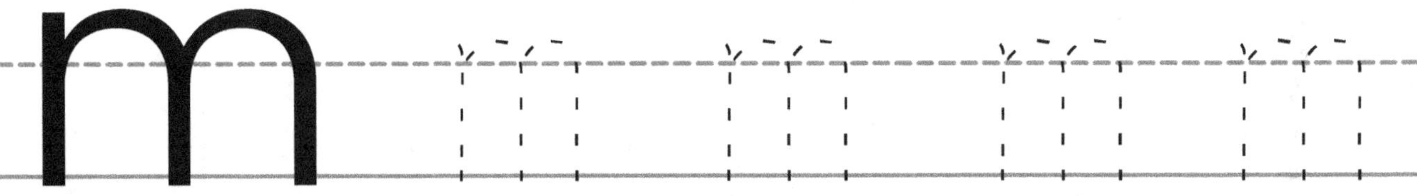

Nn

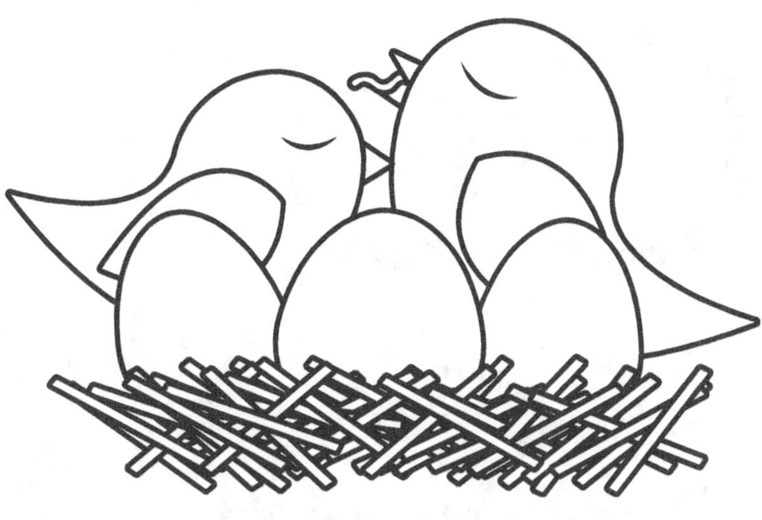

N

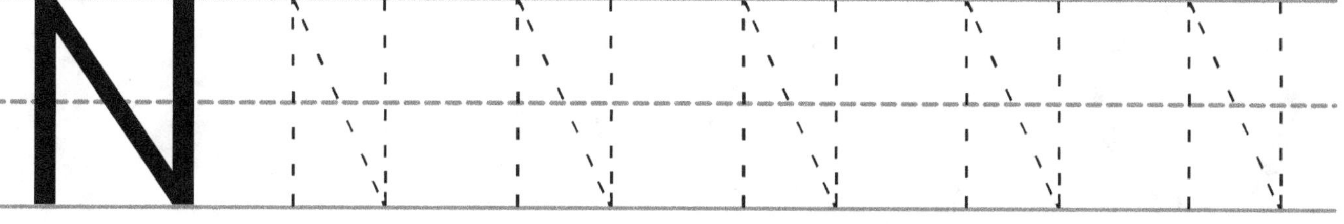

n

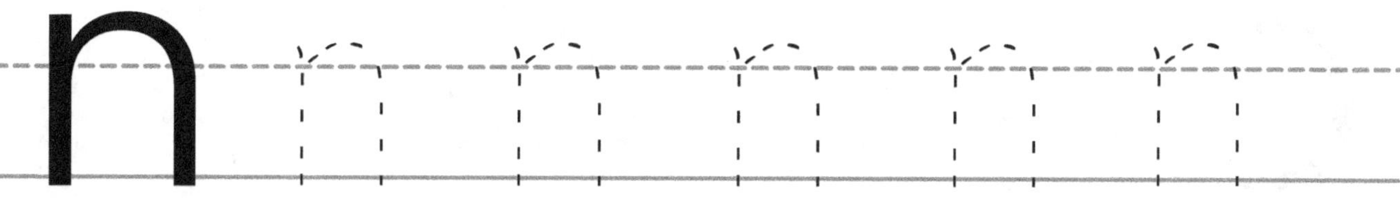

N

n

Oo
is for
Orange

Pp

is for
Penguin

P

p

P

p

Qq

is for

Queen

R r

Rainbow

S s

T t
is for

Tiger

T

t

T

t

U u

Unicorn

V v

Violoin

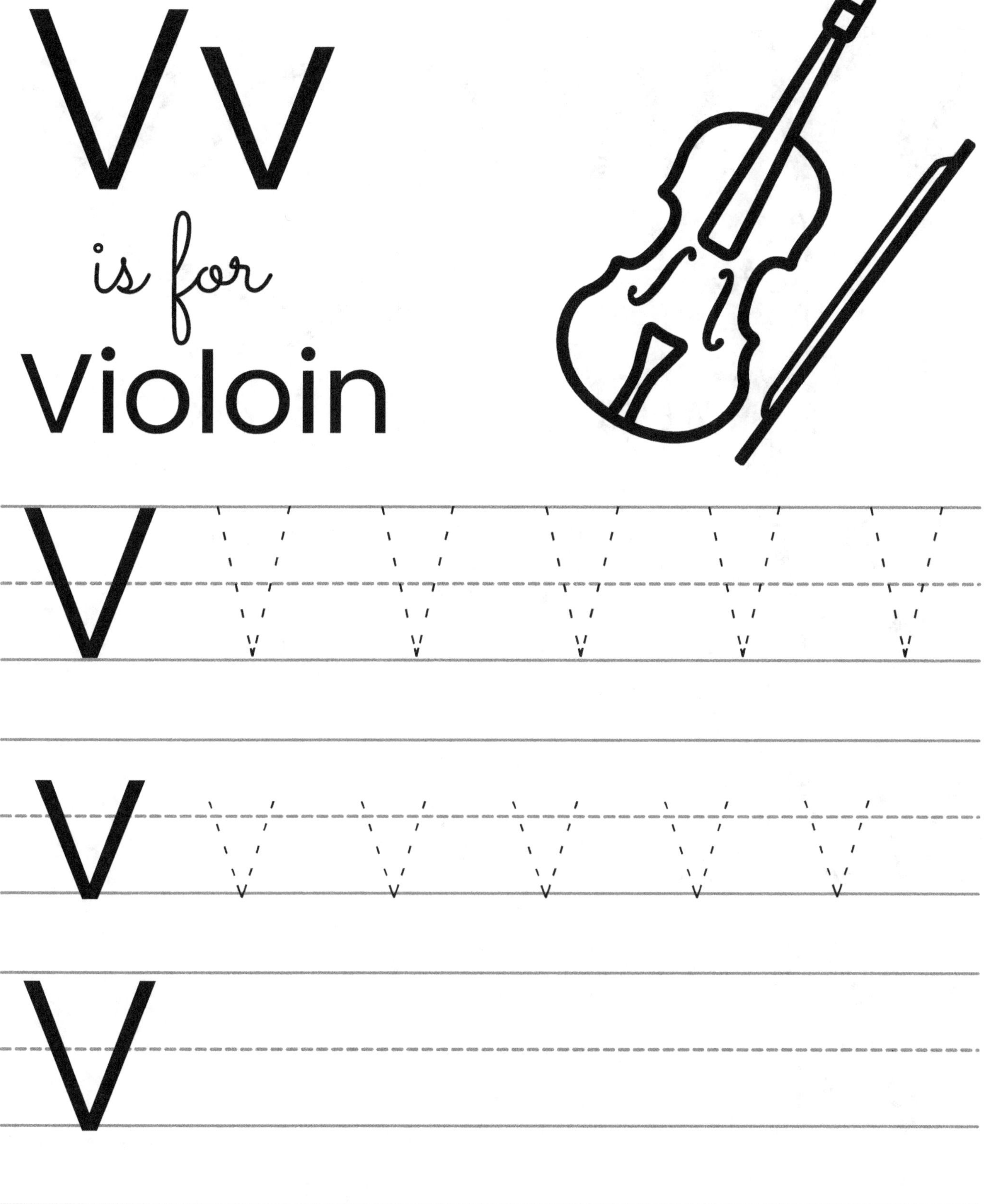

Ww

is for

Whale

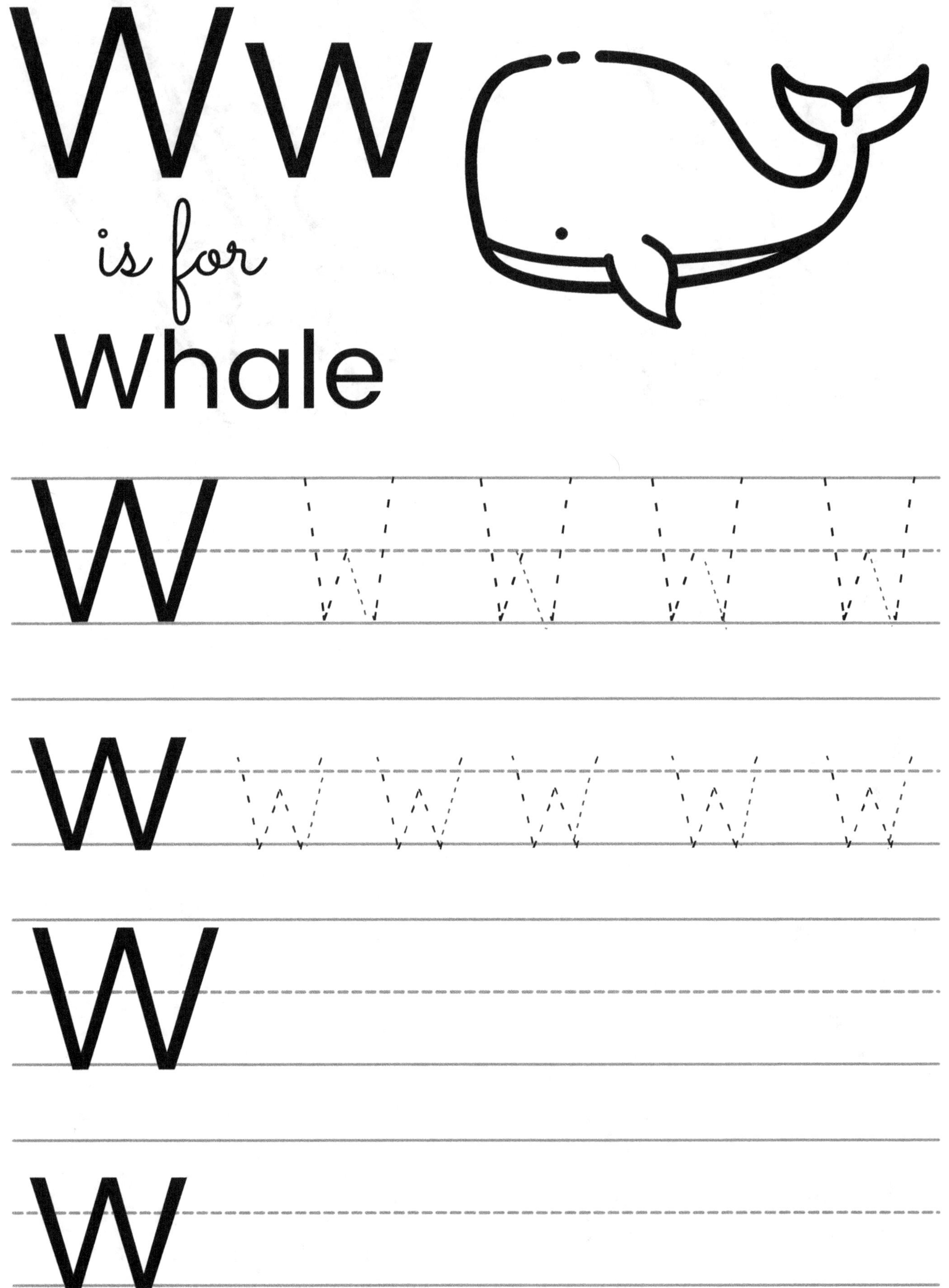

W

W

W

W

Xx

is for

X-Ray

X

X

X

X

Yy

is for

Yeti

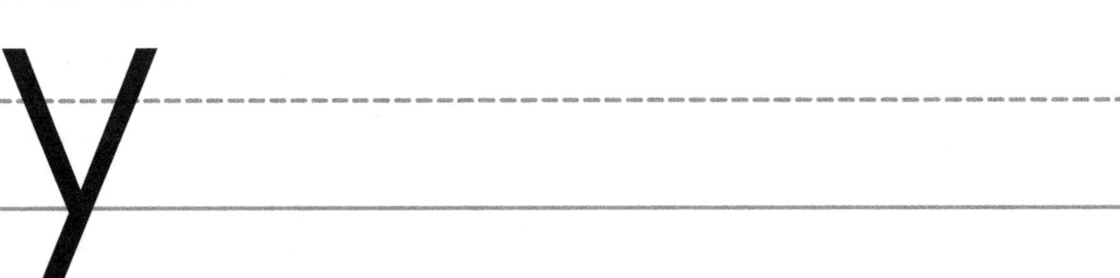

Zz

is for

Zebra

Z

z

z

z

Bonus Practice

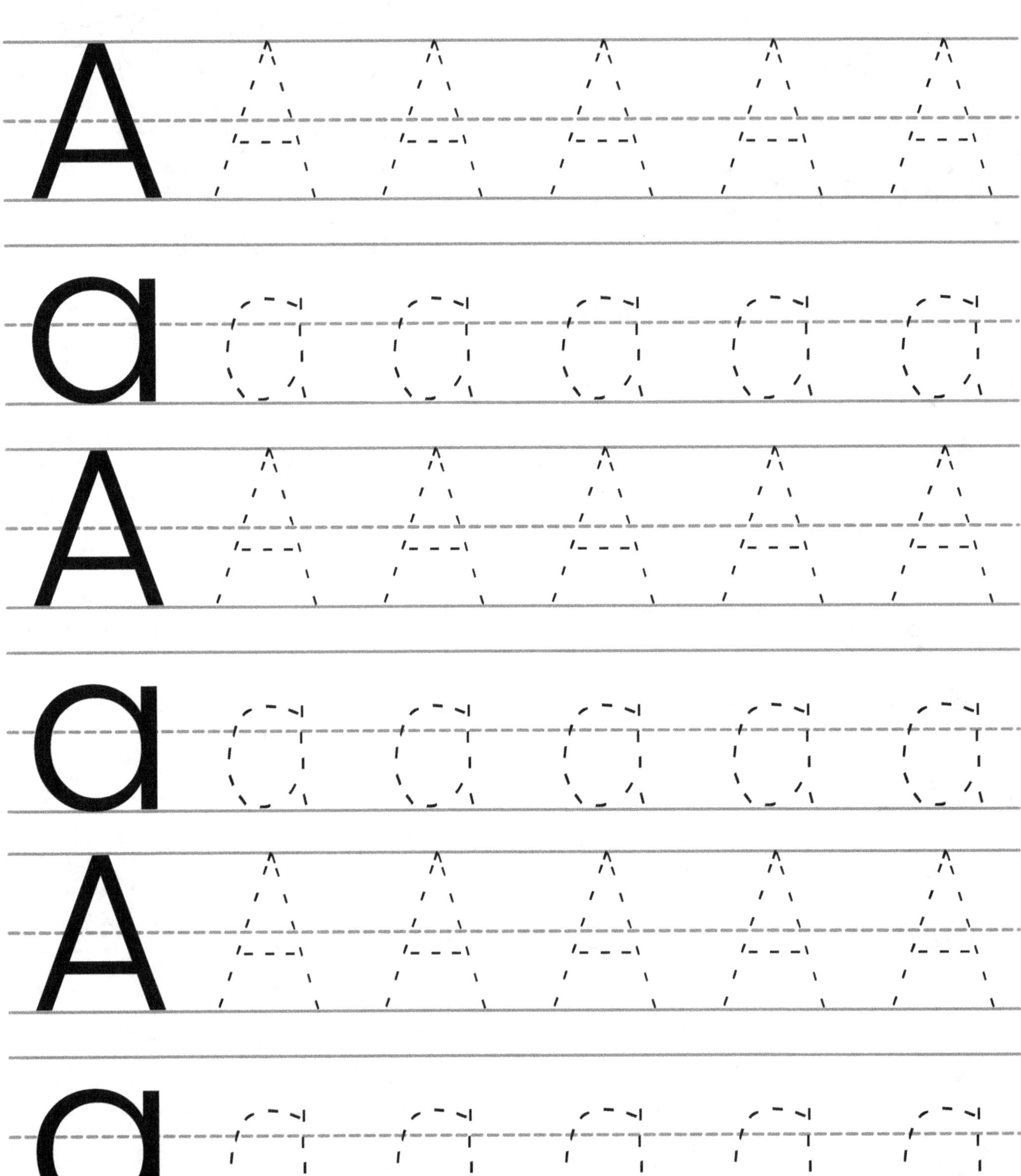

Bonus Practice

Bonus Practice

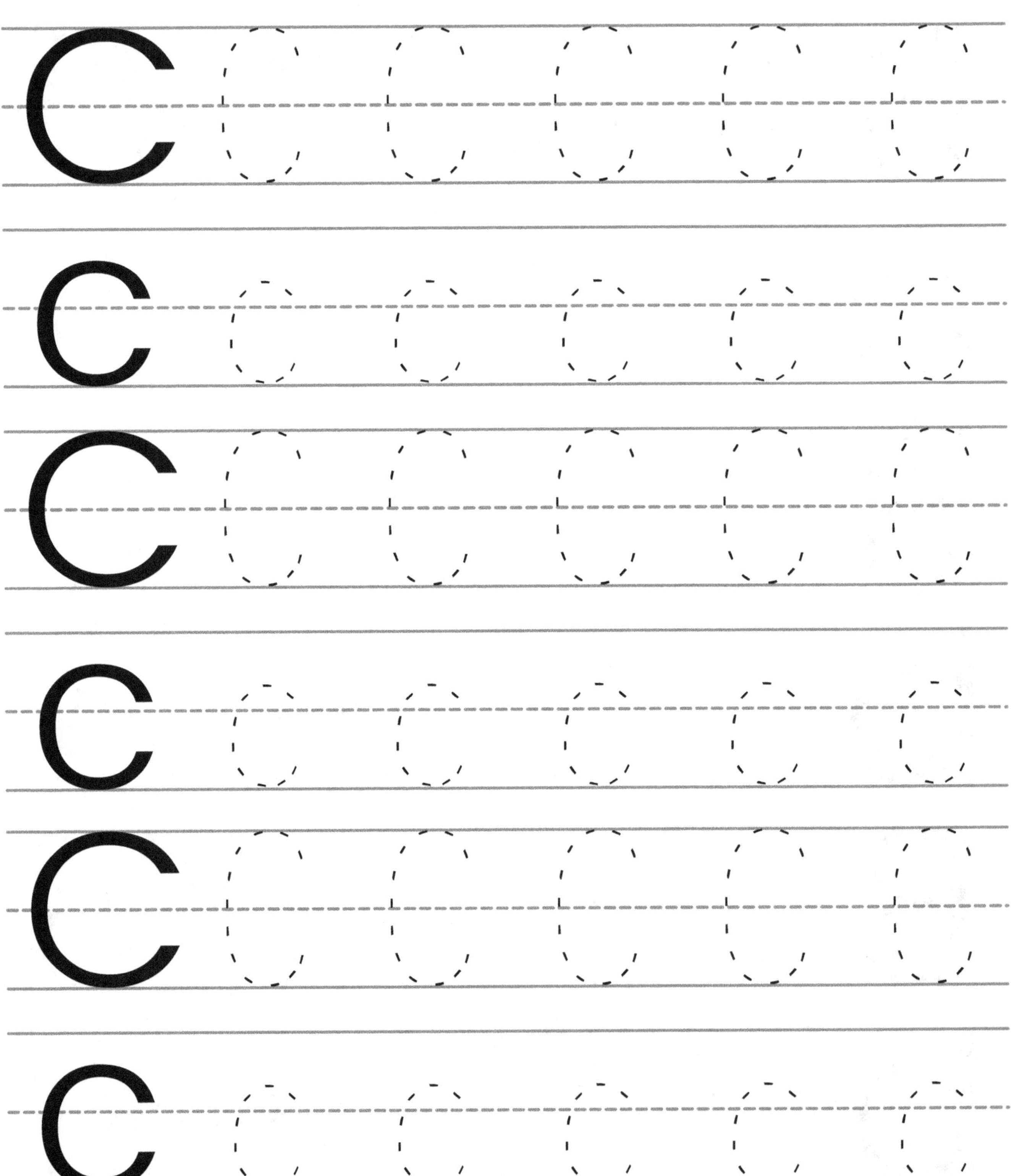

Bonus Practice

D D D D D D D D D D D

D d d d d d d d d d

D D D D D D D D D D

D d d d d d d d d d

D D D D D D D D D D

d d d d d d d d d d

Bonus Practice

Bonus Practice

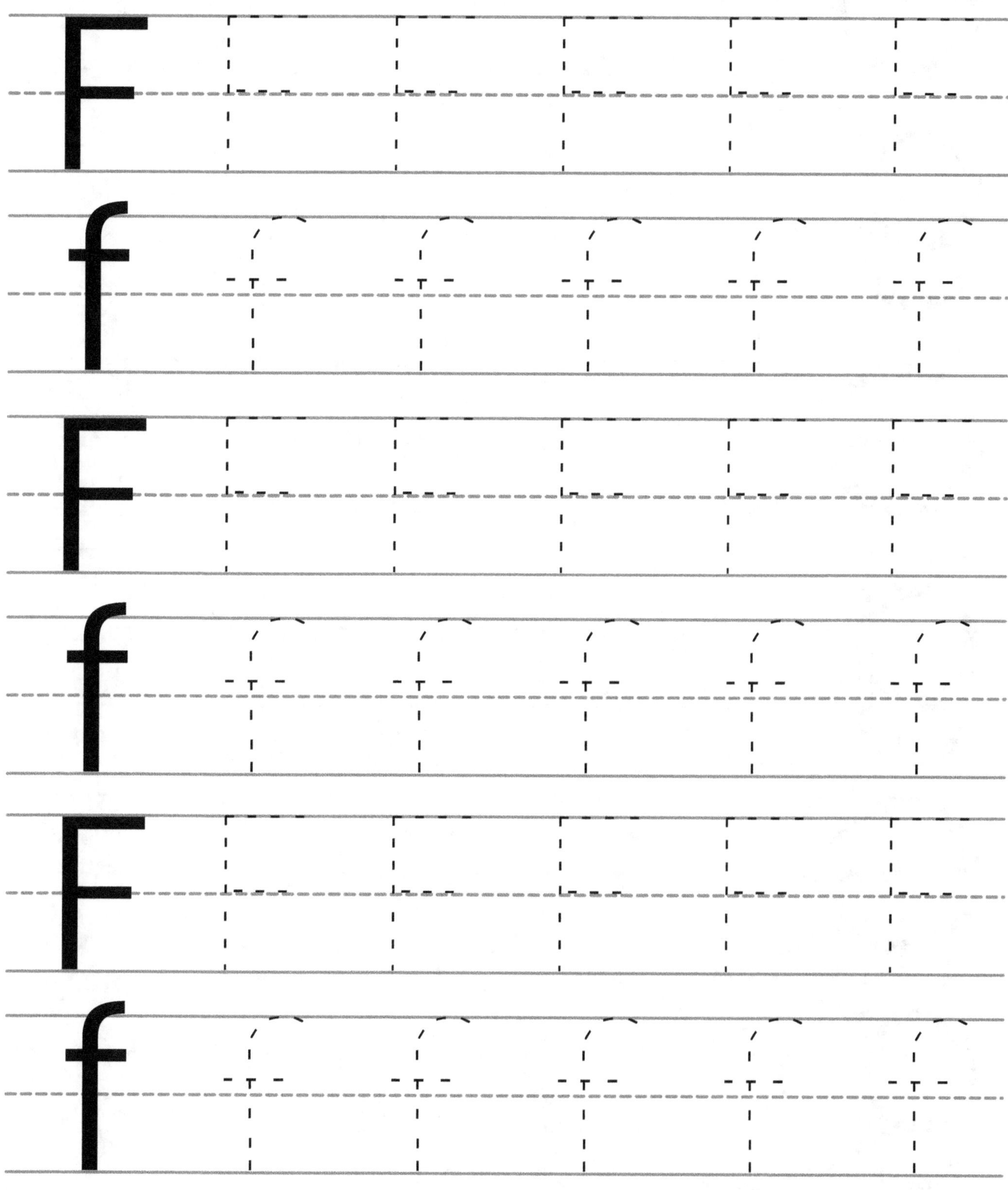

Bonus Practice

Bonus Practice

Bonus Practice

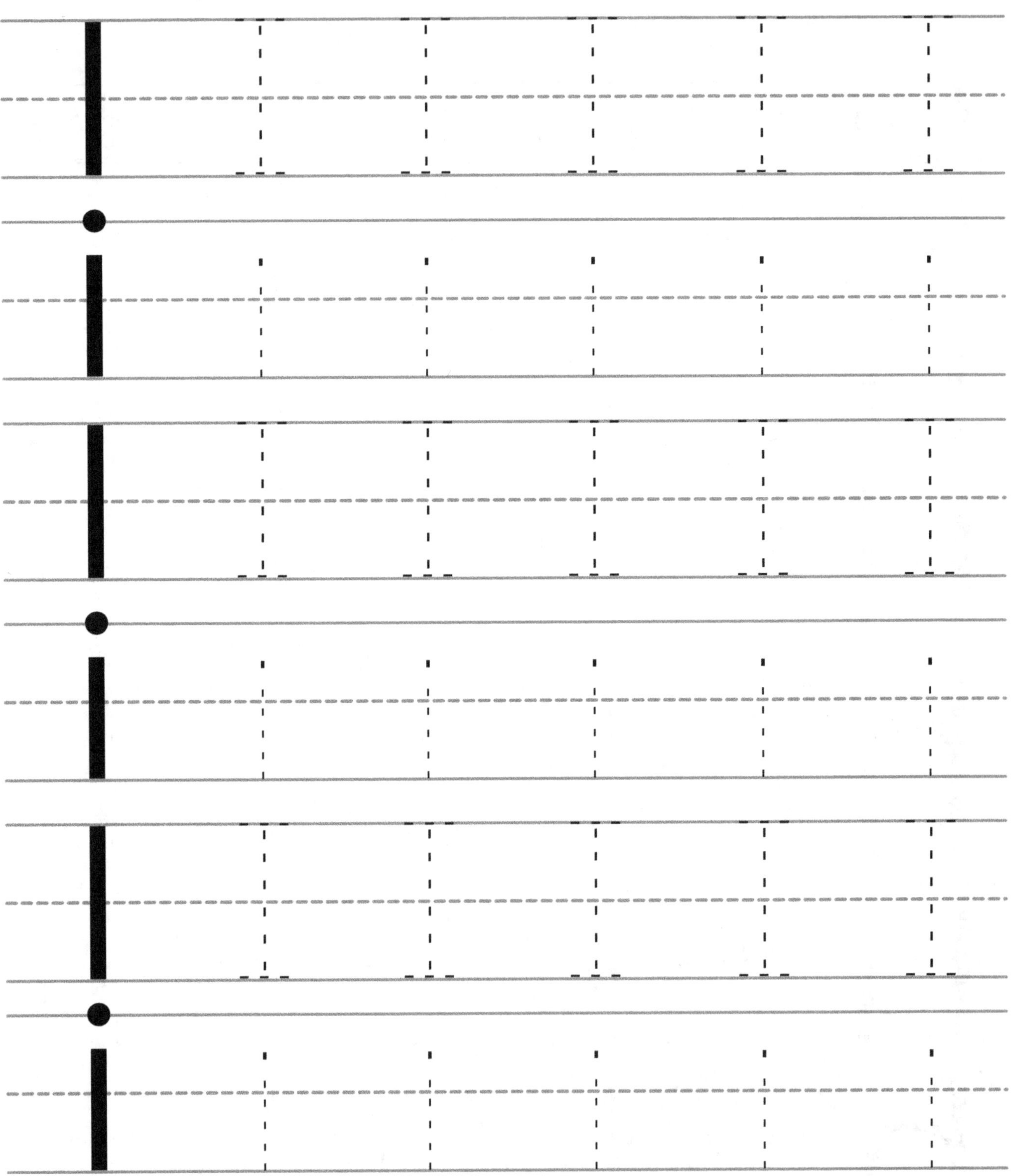

Bonus Practice

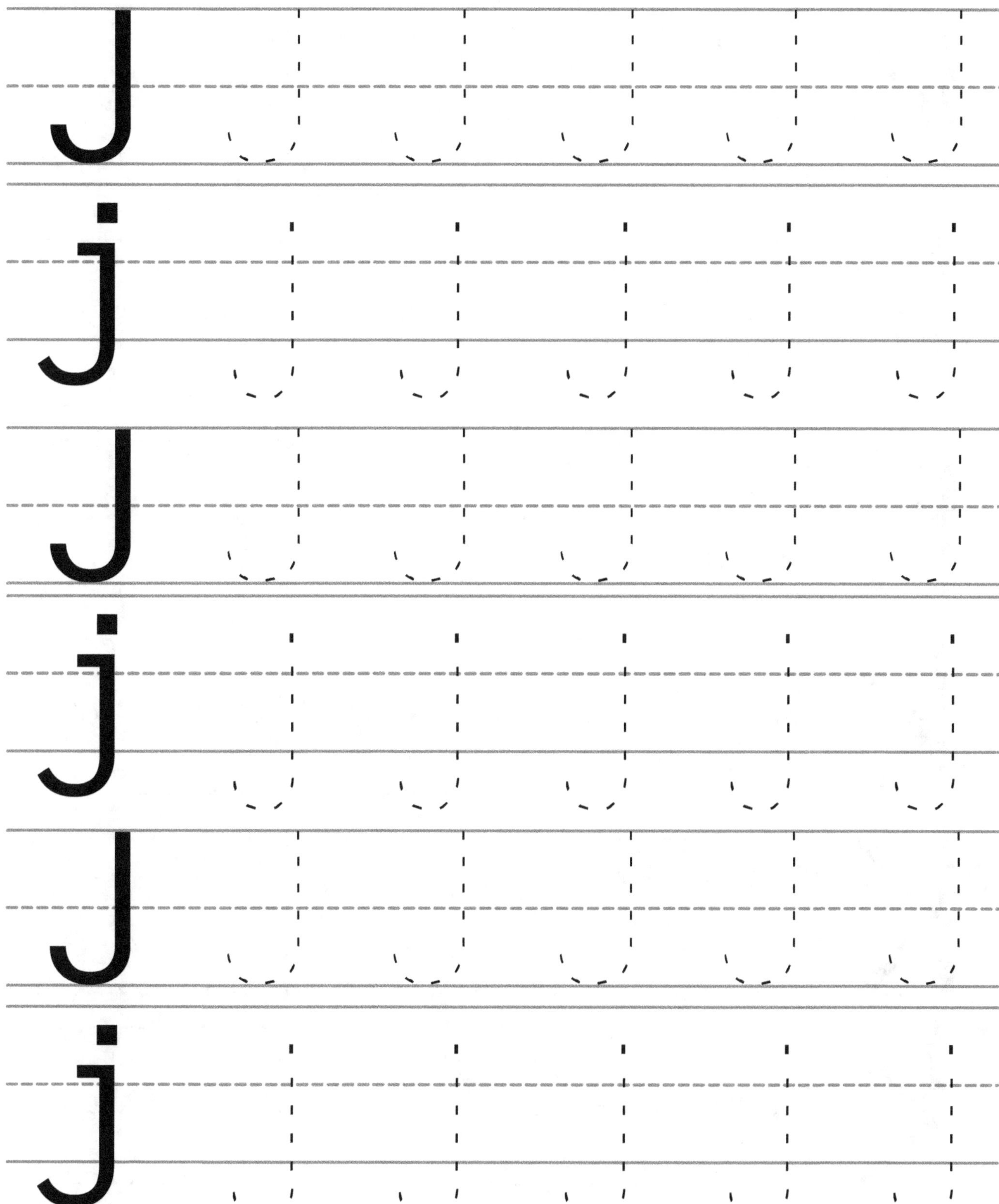

Bonus Practice

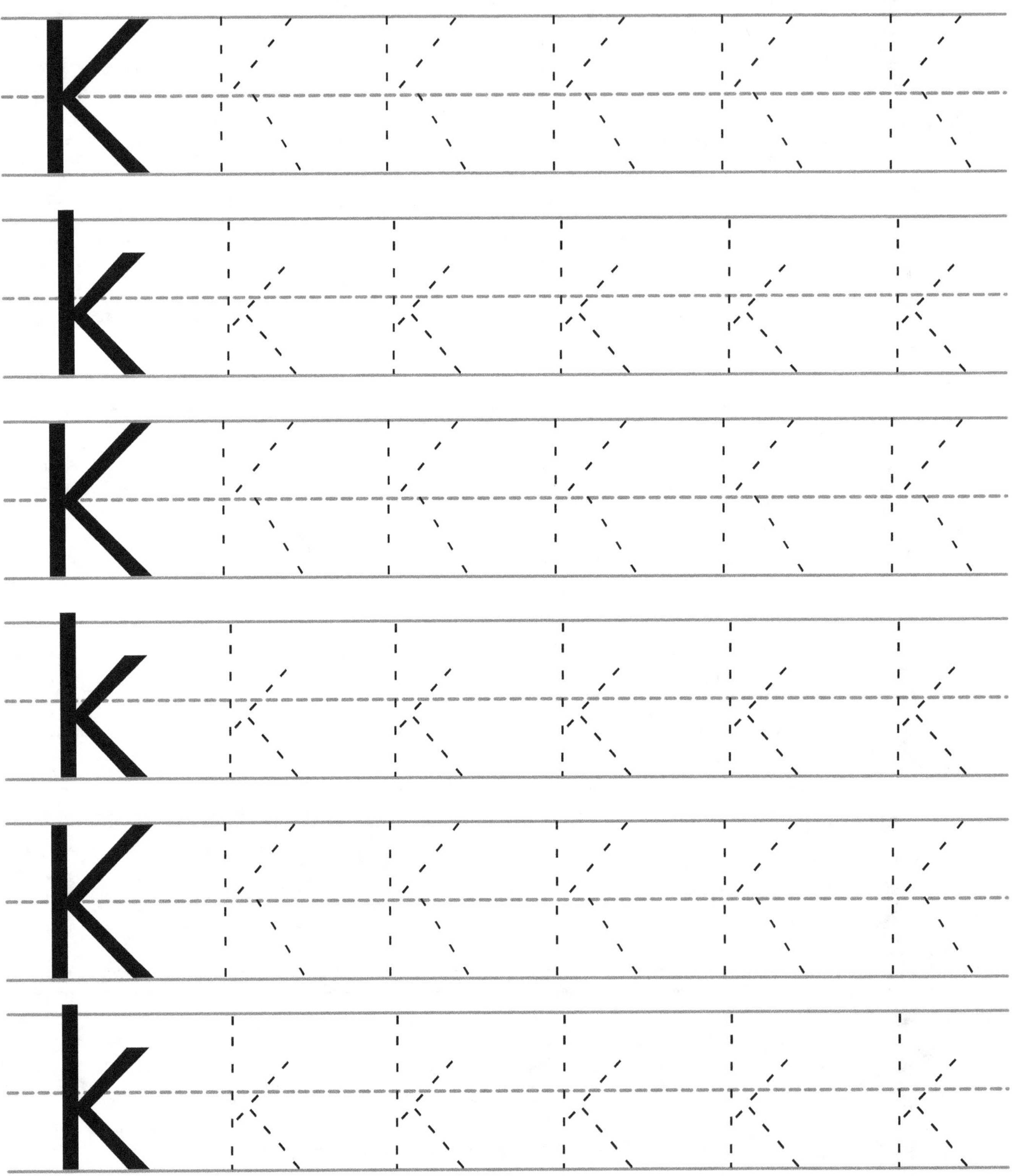

Bonus Practice

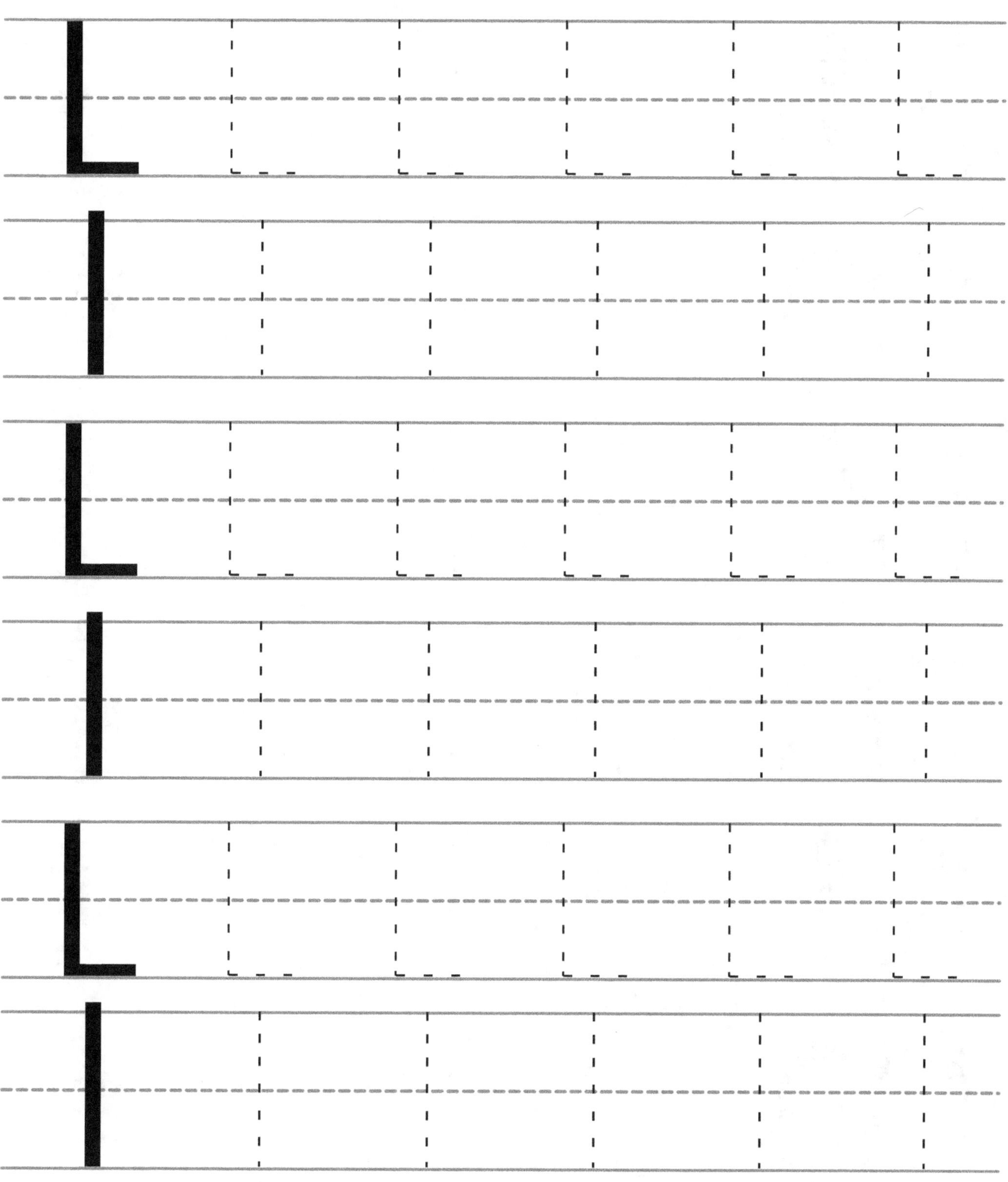

Bonus Practice

Bonus Practice

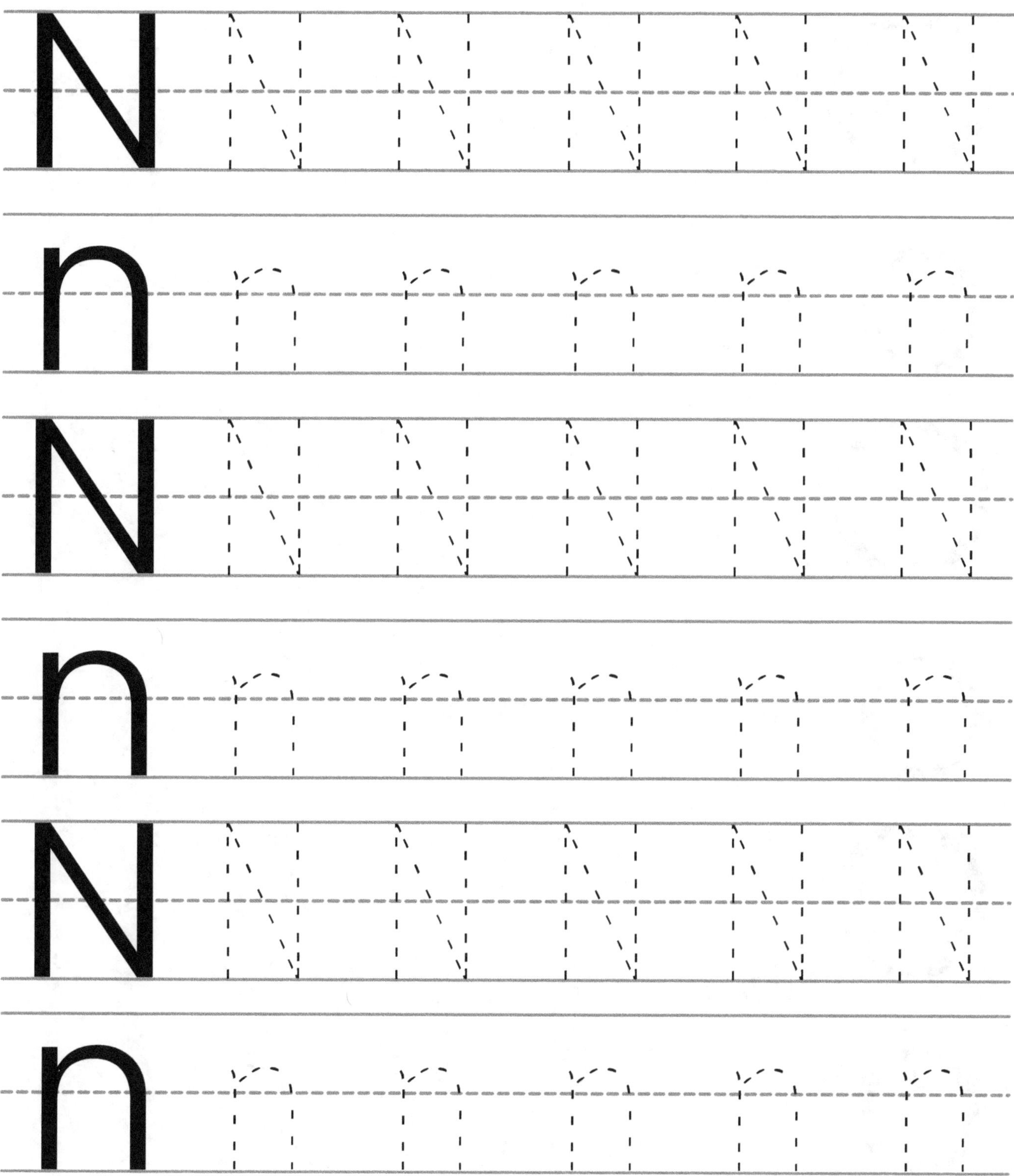

Bonus Practice

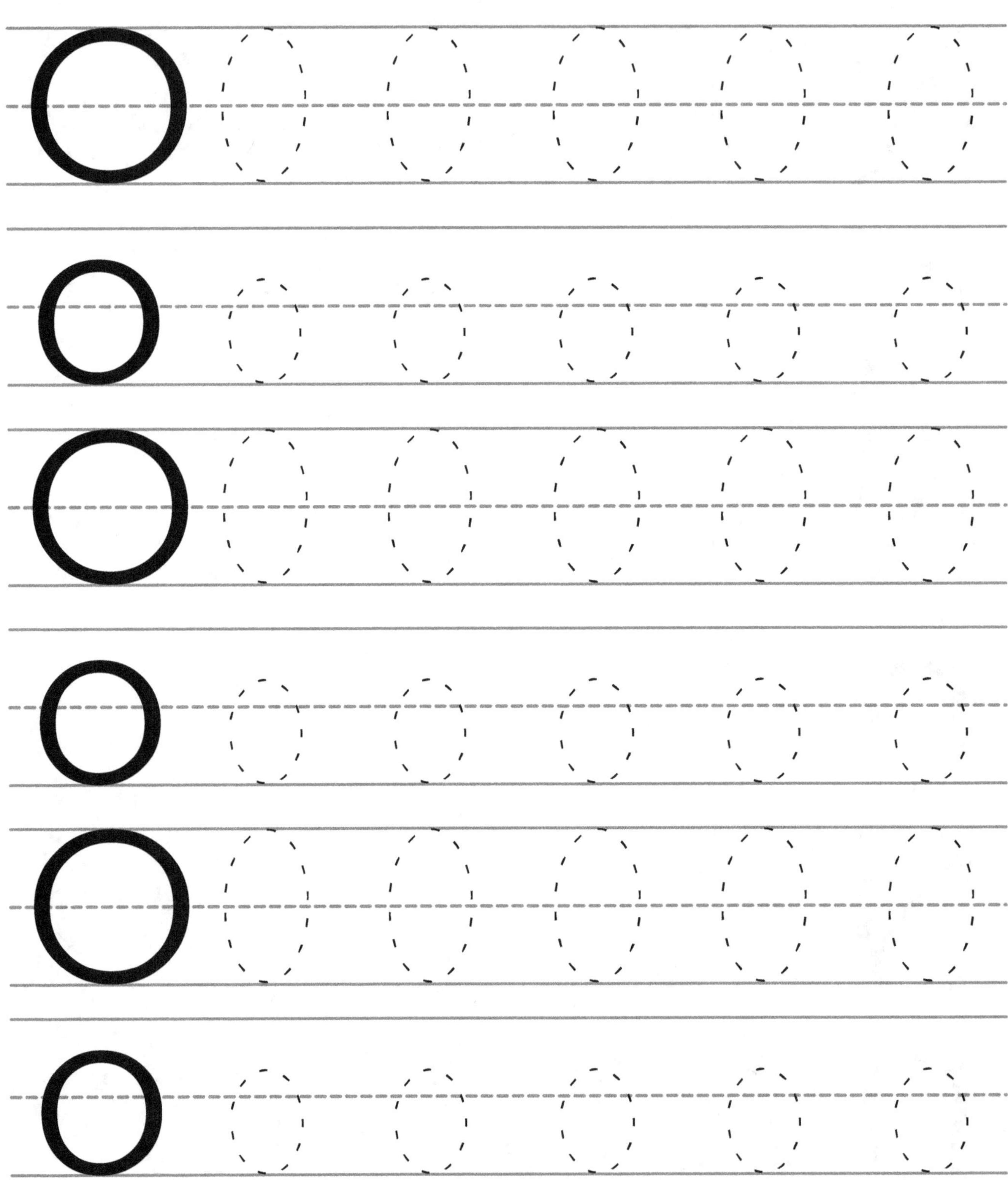

Bonus Practice

P P P P P P P

p p p p p p p

P P P P P P P

p p p p p p p

P P P P P P P

p p p p p p p

Bonus Practice

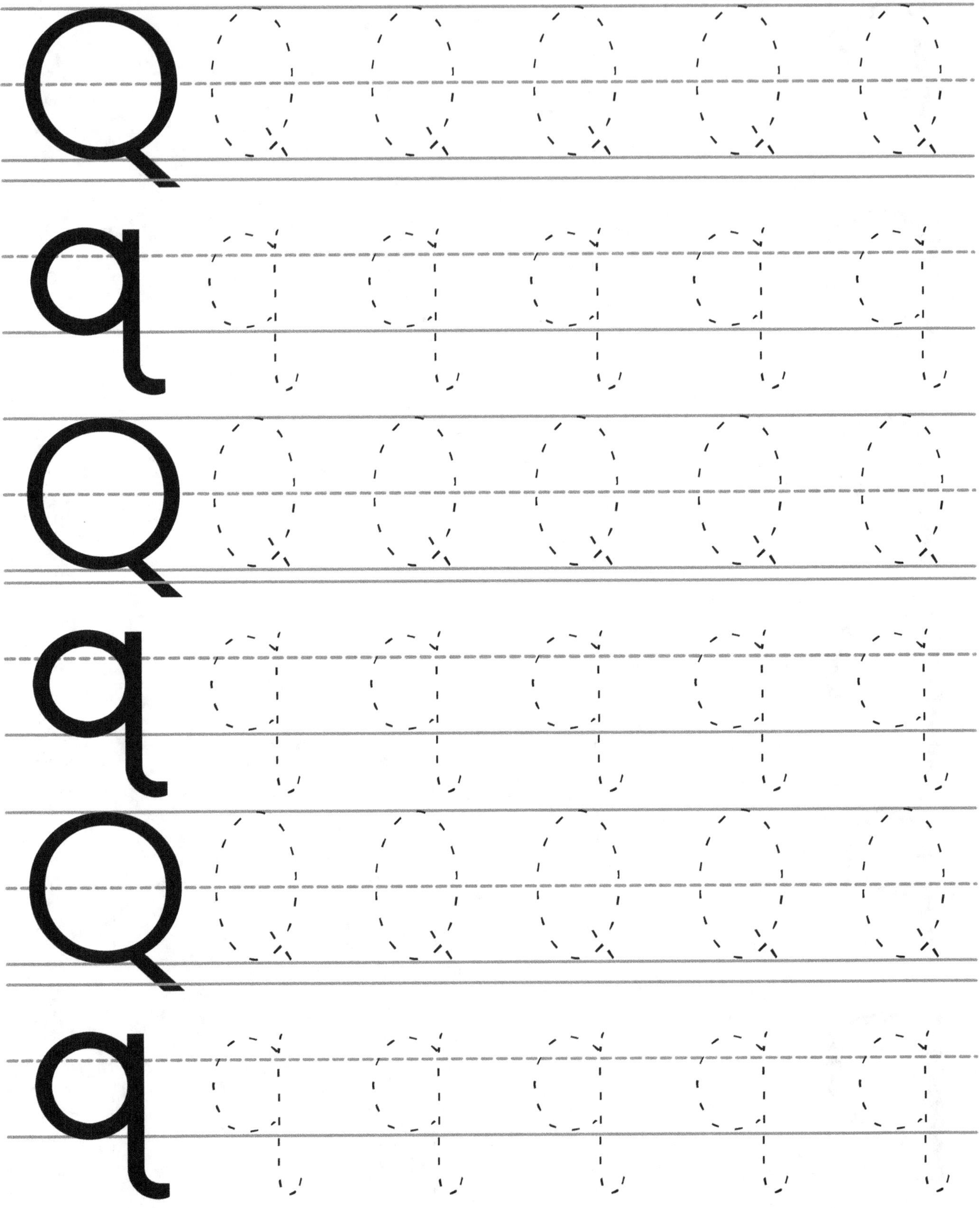

Bonus Practice

Bonus Practice

S S S S S S

S S S S S S

S S S S S S

S S S S S S

S S S S S S

S S S S S S

Bonus Practice

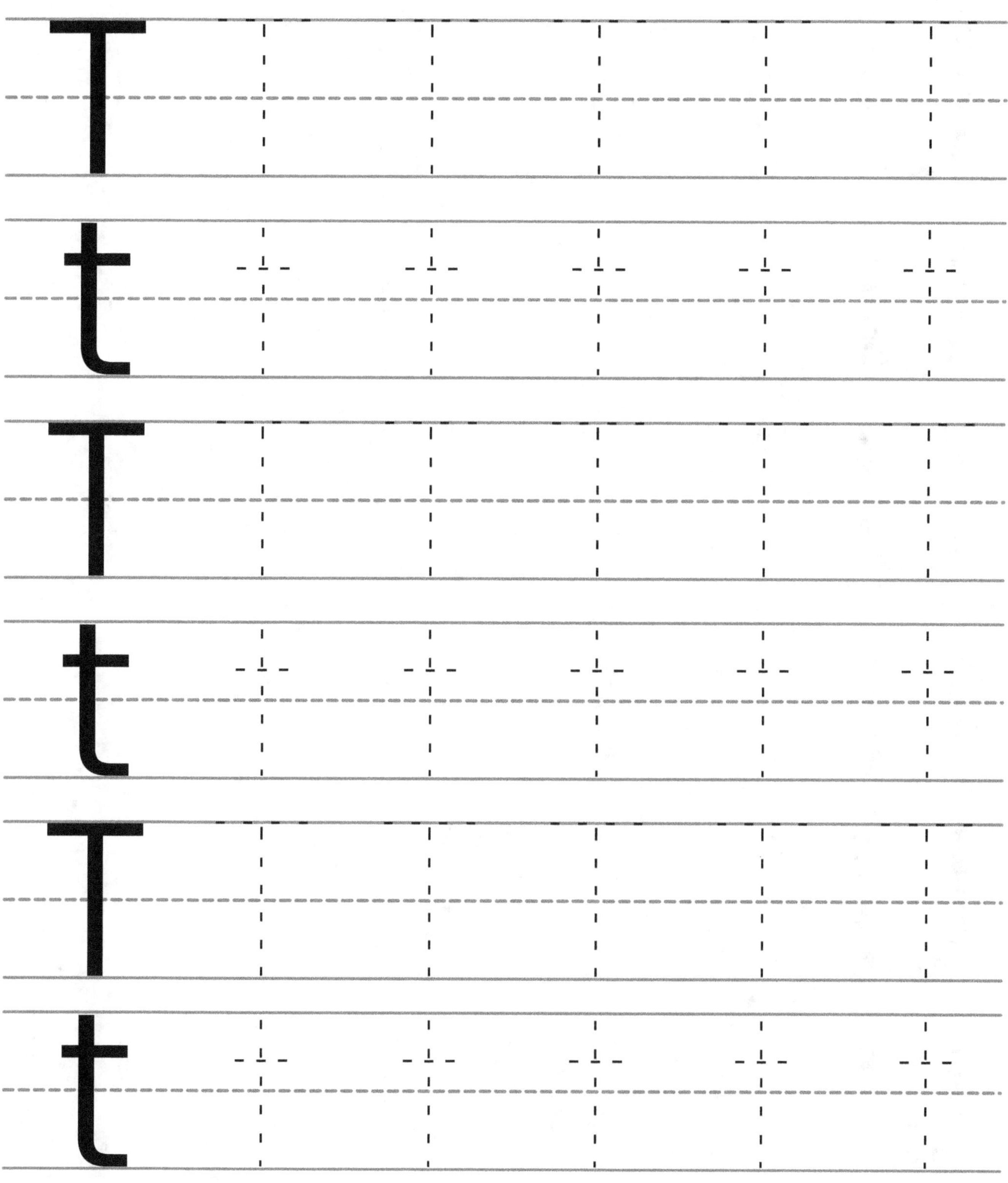

Bonus Practice

Bonus Practice

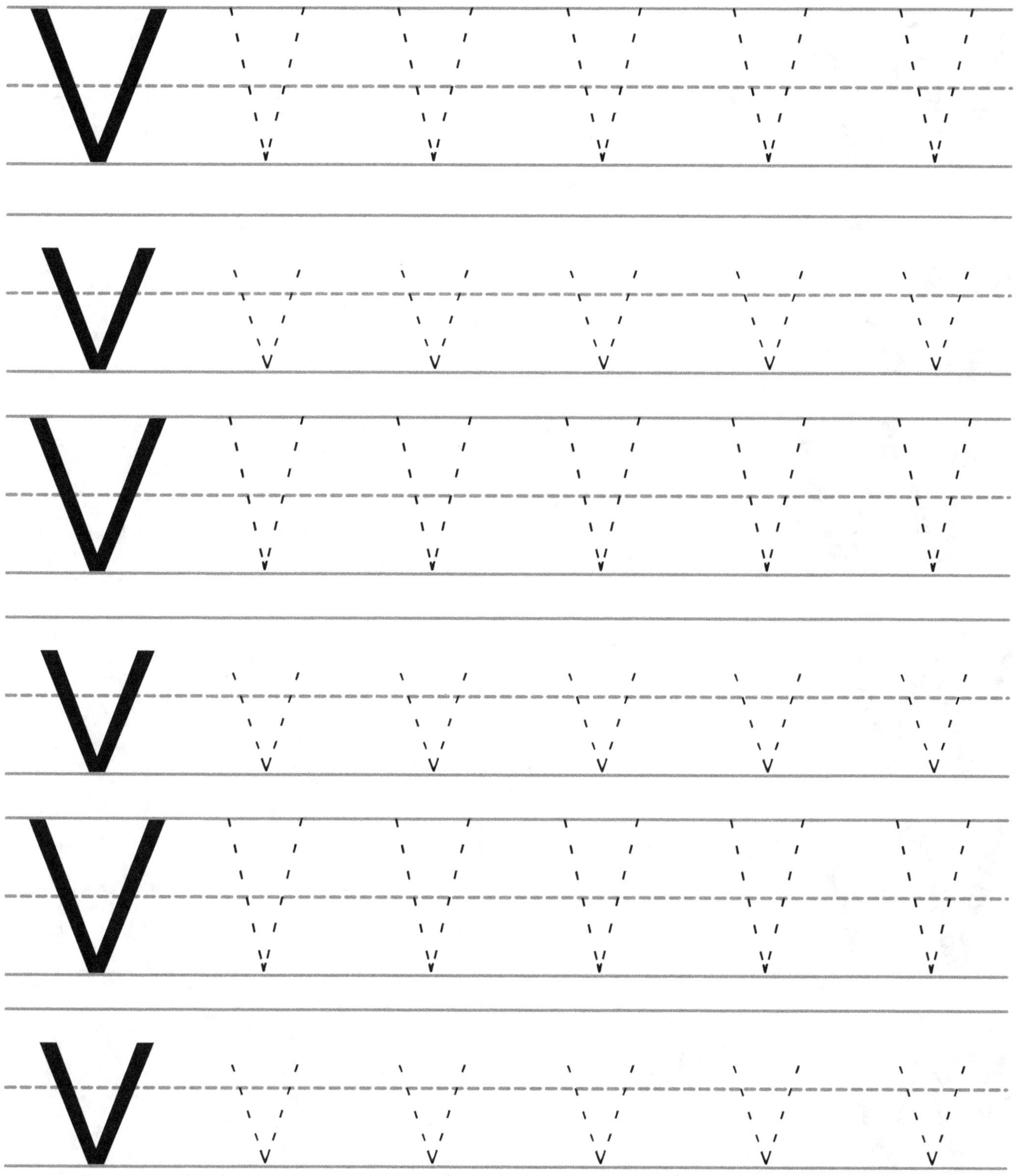

Bonus Practice

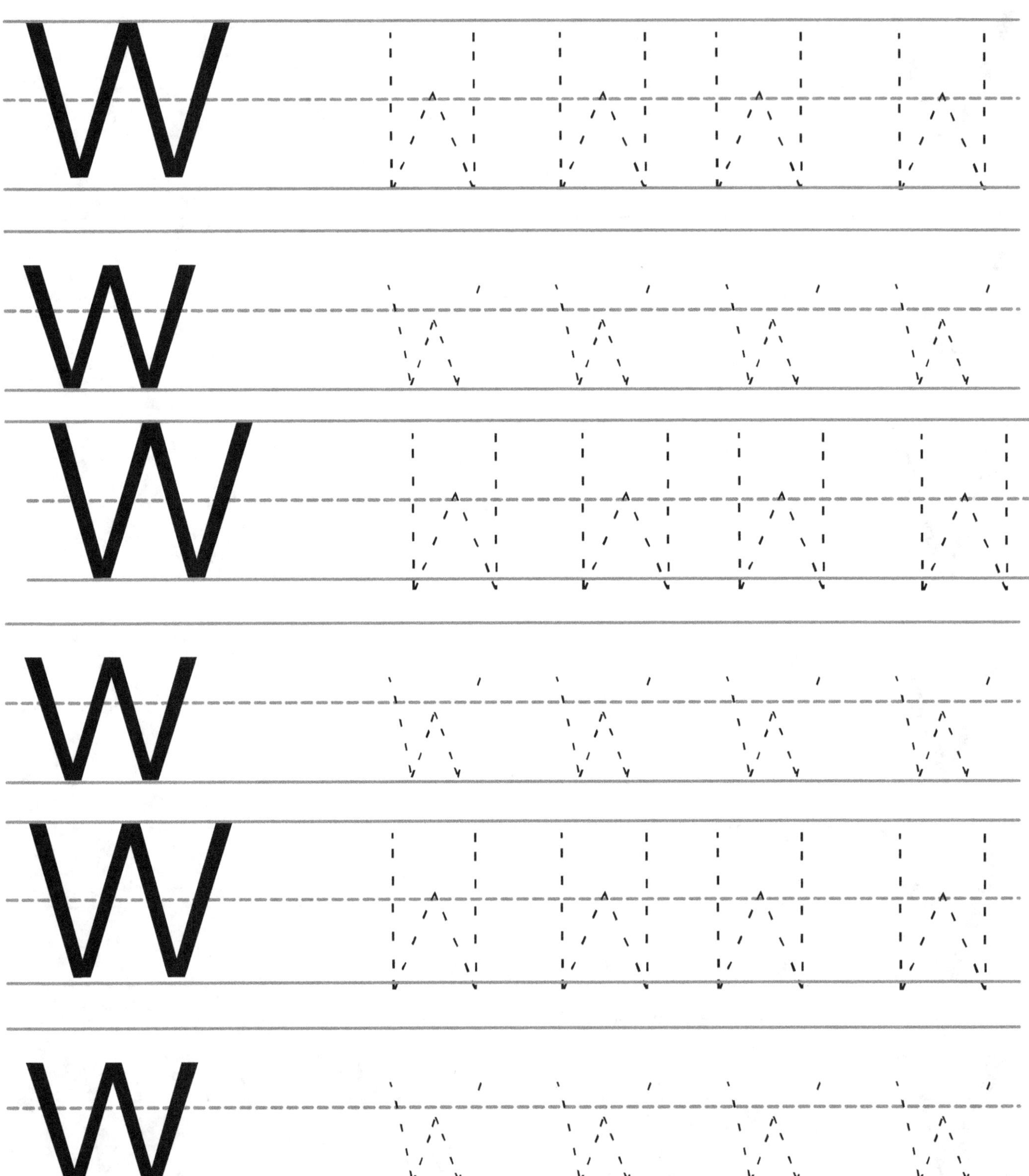

Bonus Practice

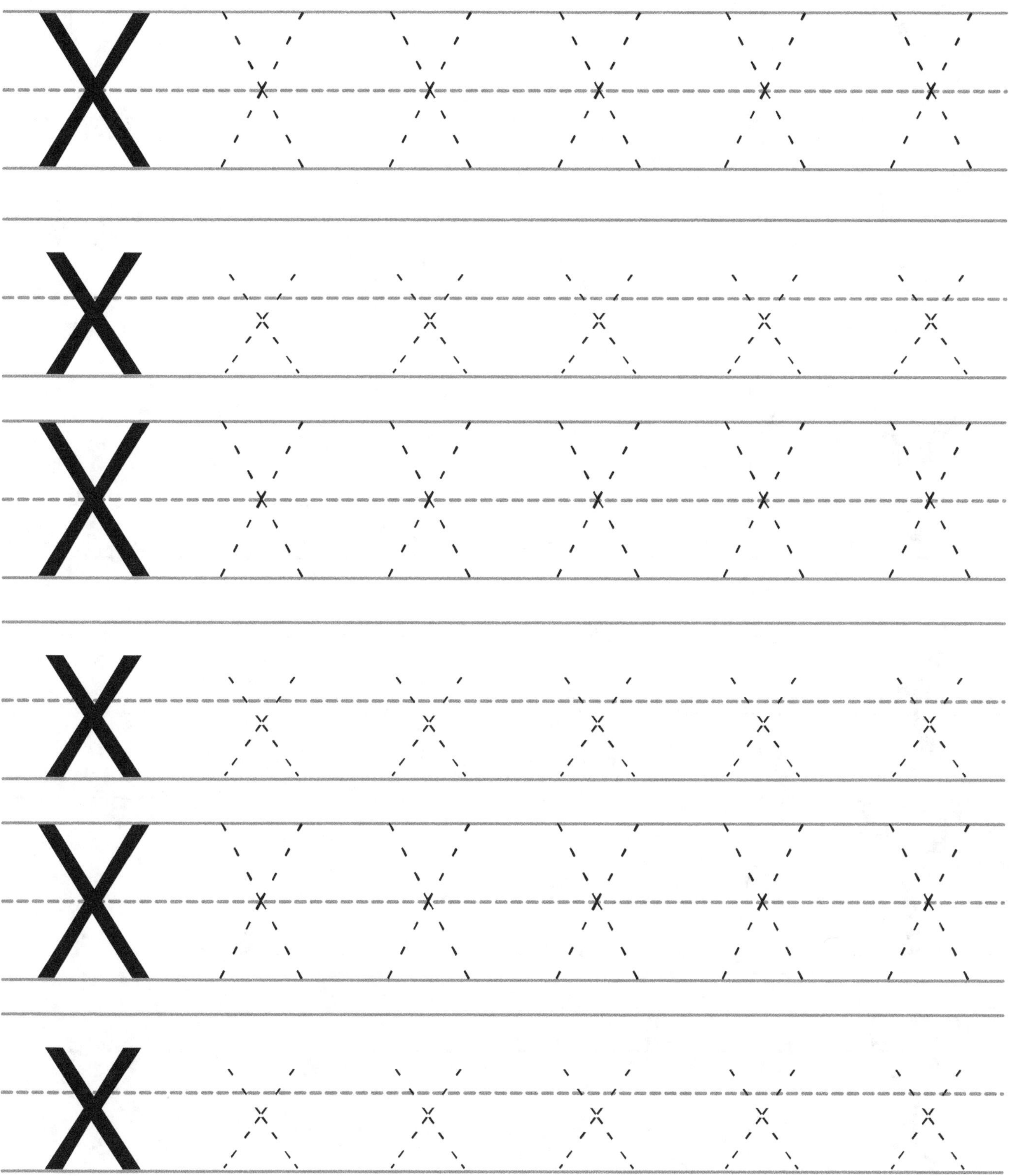

Bonus Practice

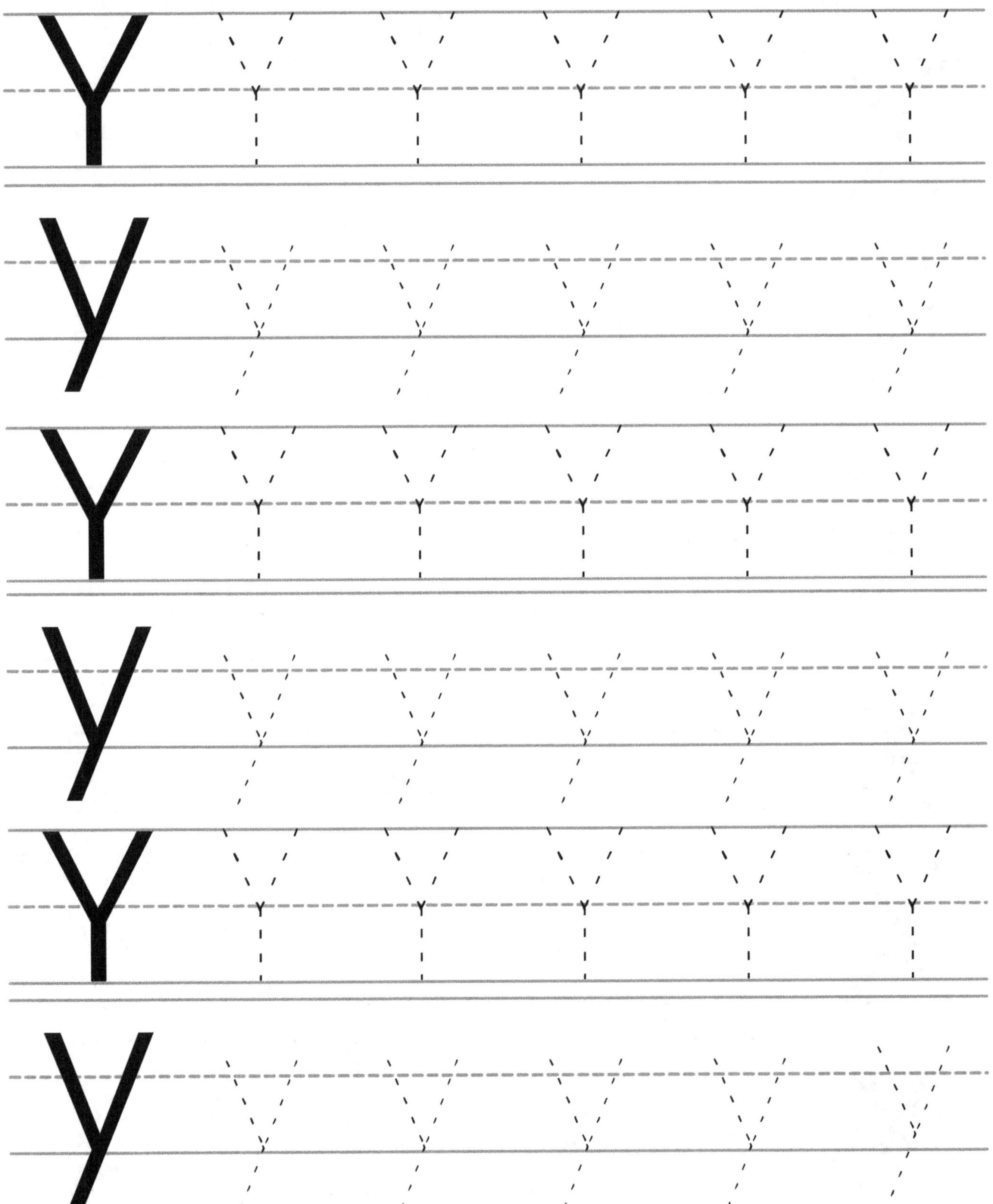

Bonus Practice

Numbers Bonus

Numbers Bonus

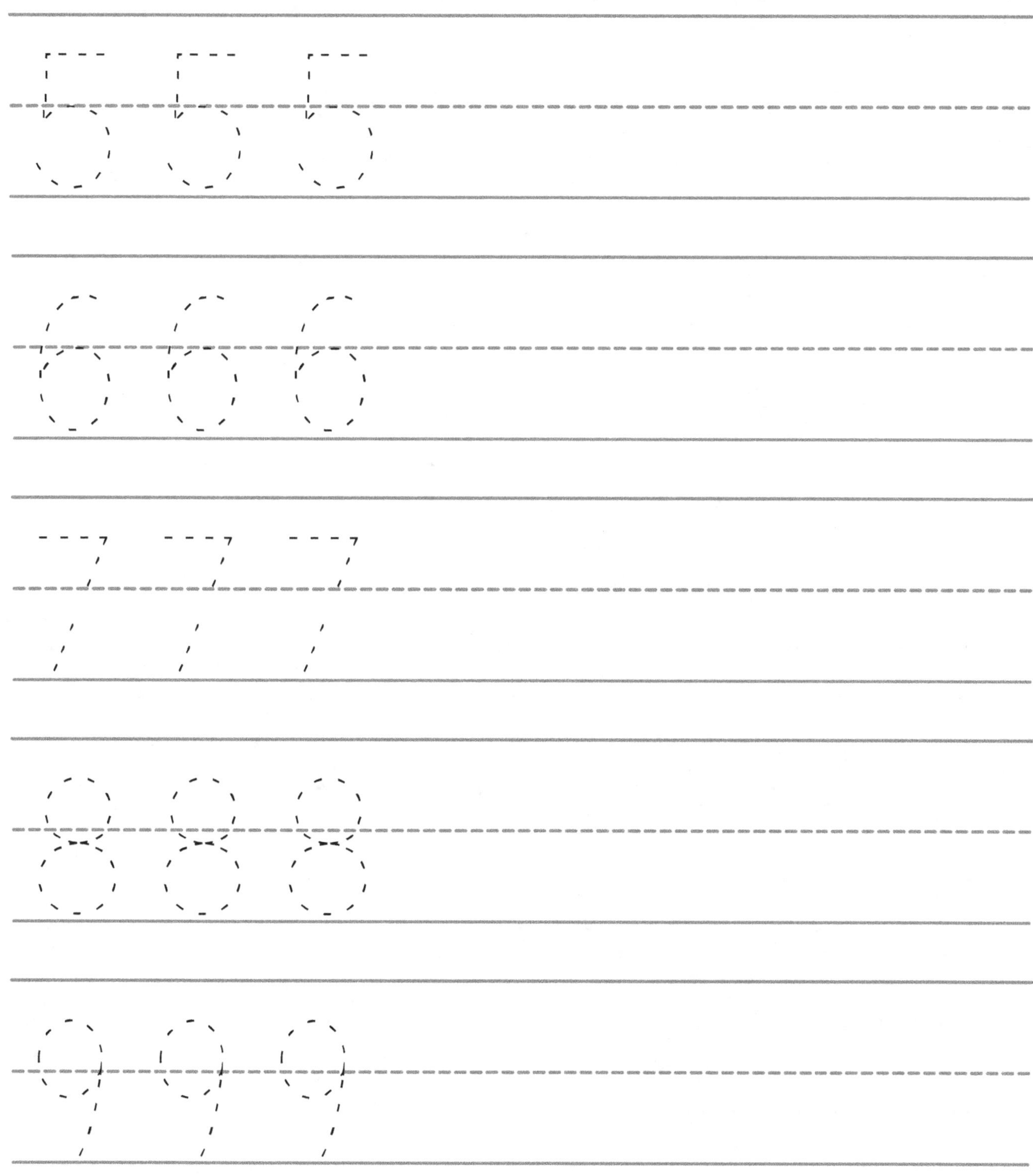

Numbers Bonus

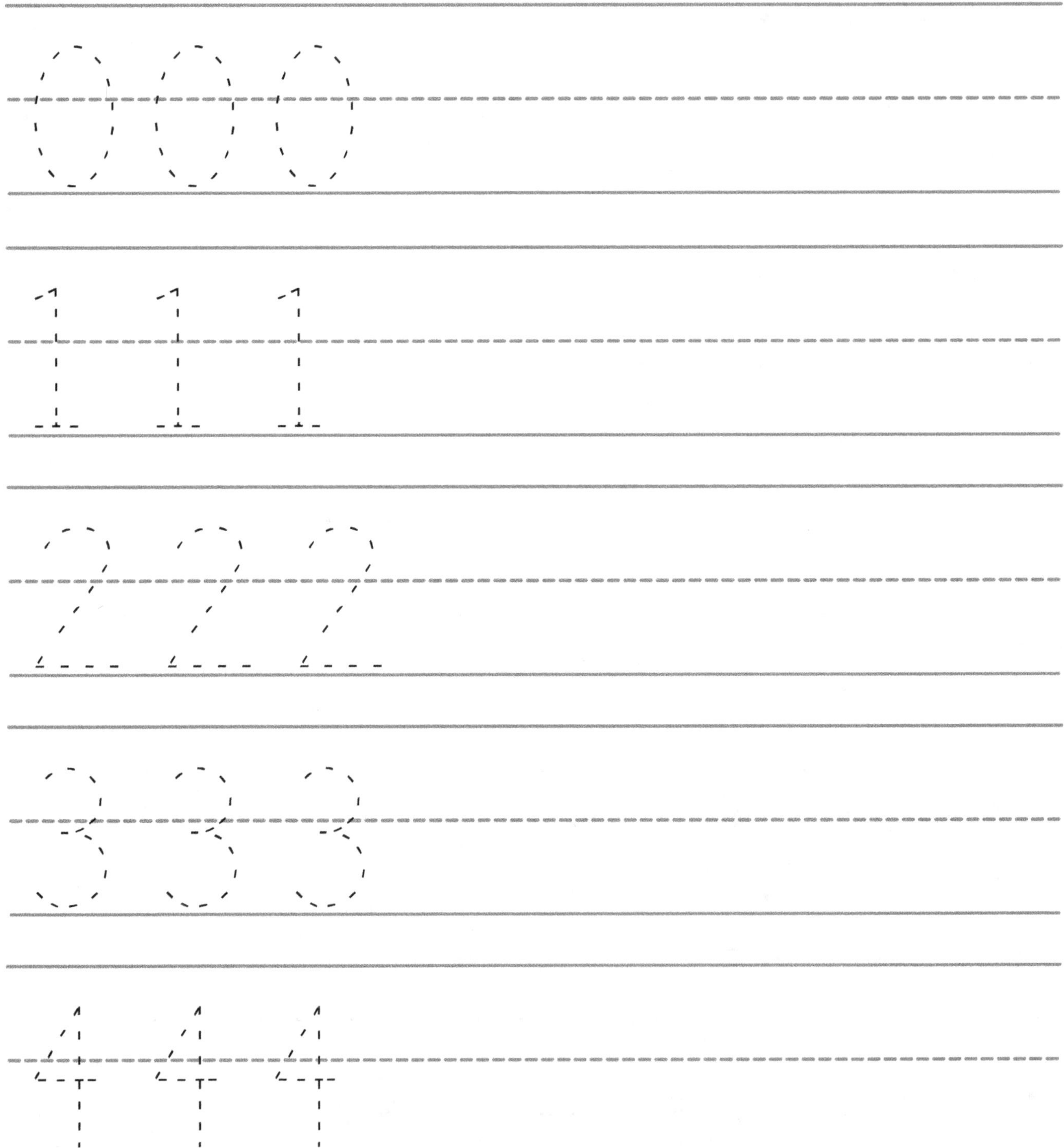

Numbers Bonus

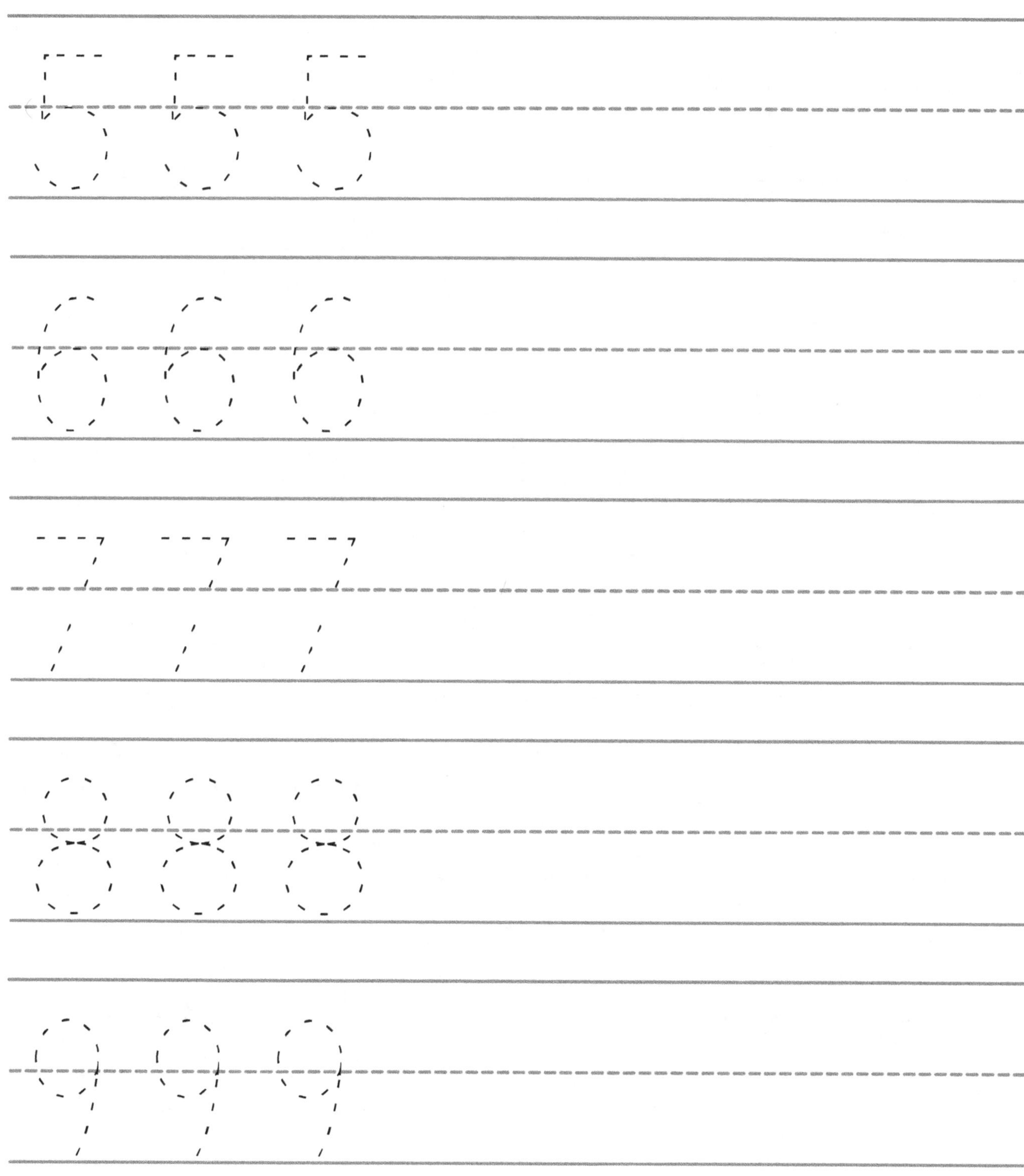

Numbers Bonus

0 0 0

1 1 1

2 2 2

3 3 3

4 4 4

Numbers Bonus

Keep an eye out for my upcoming numbers, words, & math books